MW00723906

Hand Me My Griot Clothes

Hand Me My Griot Clothes
The Autobiography of Junior Baby

Peter J. Harris

DuForcelf

Hand Me My Griot Clothes

Copyright ©1993 by Peter J. Harris

All Rights Reserved

No part of this publication may be reproduced or transmitted in any form or by any means, without written permission.

Chapter 5 has appeared in *Nommo, An OBAC Anthology of Contemporary Black Writing*, 1990.

Chapter 10 has appeared in *Konceptualizations*, vol. 8, no. 2.

A DuForcelf book published by
Black Classic Press, 1993

Library of Congress Catalog Card No.: 91-74132

ISBN 0-933121-78-4

Cover design by Carles Juzang

Photograph by Seán Bennett

Printed on acid free paper to assure long life

Founded in 1978, Black Classic Press specializes in bringing to light obscure and significant works by and about people of African descent. If our books are not available in your area, ask your local bookseller to order them. Our current list of titles can be obtained by writing:

Black Classic Press
c/o List
P.O. Box 13414
Baltimore, MD 21203-3414

A Young Press With Some Very Old Ideas

for Daddy

for Richard (Mr. Dick) Wilson

also

for the men of Parklands in Southeast

Daddy: I finally understand what you mean by,

"You can't have your cake and eat it too...."

Griots are Africa's "living documents with the gifts of speech," according to the late Guinean writer Camara Laye. "Guardian of the Word" is Laye's description of these oral historians, whose memories link the present with the past through "chants, epics and legends." With Junior Baby, I hope to honor the griot's desire to "serve the word and the world beyond the word," as Laye put it. I pray that Junior Baby wears his sacred clothes with a style that's timeless and hip on all sides of the ocean.

Peter J. Harris

CONTENTS

Chapter 1
That Day Was A New Year

Junior Baby nodding out front of his tv set
jerk awake when the newsman
switch from weather sports & national news
to a happy new year story in Virginia
two trashmen stopped at a roadblock
made of $4,000 in cash
gave it back to the owner
one Homeboy say:
yeah...our friends called us fools...
his Walkboy say:
I am a down to earth guy. I'm honest.
I don't believe in beating nobody
out of nothing...
Junior Baby question his own heart
turn off the tv
get up & click on his tape recorder
begin the first chapter
of his autobiography
HAND ME MY GRIOT CLOTHES
start dictating:

Y ou can't *plan* on getting to
become a Breathtaking Nigger
can't straight-line outline or
train your mind to sit people up
so they find themselves in you
you can't study steady burning midnight oils or
hold court counting your cash
to touch another man's heart, soul & mind

it's like making love
you can't *talk* up no real true loving

can't just dictate what touch make
a woman jump & purr
I know
I had to learn
it take an Open Nature
make a woman sing her own sweet song
that was a hard lesson for somebody
looking good as I looked in my younger days
I could have been Zorro if I was Mexican
swooping in on a snorting stallion
swinging down on a bee's waxed lifeline
land a standing man ready for scandal
calamity fun fighting or saving the day
land a high stepping man on any dance floor in town
outshimmy
hold my drink
doing it to death until I caught the eye
of everybody in the joint

still it took real love
to let me know
I needed permission to be a breathtaking lover
met this woman
so fine she didn't leave footprints
stayed dry in rainstorms
& answered my questions with whipped cream whispers
she like me right off
but kept hold her best self
until I hung up my cape outside &
traded my sword for a magic wand
(she did let me save a little stallion)

she took my hands
put all my fingers on her shoulders
showed me how to take my time
her skin was the definition of smooth
the longer I lingered

the louder hope hummed between us
when I finally got the hang of it
sound like we was joined by Christmas carols
we was hymns stroked & shouted soulful by
some group like the Dixie Hummingbirds
that's when I learned you don't have
to breathe to really breathe
that air come in your body
through touching somebody you love
I learned to be myself & ignore whatever
my buddies in the peanut gallery had on their minds

she the one called me a Breathtaking Nigger
in her real voice making my stallion rear up & gallop
running hot & cold chills up my spine & out my eyes
looking into her best self

hand me my griot clothes
cause when them boys hauled that money
back without concern wish or wonder
about reward the first
I heard voices from two new
Breathtaking Niggers
& learned how to breathe all over again

there they was standing with that sweet dip
good men bring to friendly side by side
compactor truck parked behind them
hat in hand stroking a worker's beard
who would have thought two trashmen
could be the downbeat kicking off a 21st Century
style of schooling all who want to do the right thing
who would have thought we find a wisdom
swinging like Count Basie's band
from the drawl of Virginia trash haulers
saying yeah

we may not got the most glamour on our gig
but that don't mean we don't know right from wrong

hand me my griot clothes
that day was a new year
I smell dew on the new year
listening to them boys giving themselves
permission to breathe deep & stand out
from the crowd like a good woman gave
me permission to be myself

they didn't plan on taking my breath away
waking up this morning at 5 a.m.
shoving on them crusty blue jeans & brogans
feeling that flannel sliding
across their backs like my hands in the
best of my dreams

they didn't count on nothing but beating that
clock enough to cool out after the pickup run
maybe go half on a half-pint or rummage
some still good used item
from the Hefty bags or cashing a check
& putting something down on a new pair
of khaki pants at the mall

until they found that bank bag
full of crab house cash
that's when Jesse Carter gave
Gregory Hayes permission & vice versa
that's when they said it was alright
to live with conscience
maybe not rich
but definitely not poor

Junior Baby turn off the tape recorder
push the rewind button
feel something under his foot
bend to pick up a 1974 penny
open the front door
flip it up in the air for good luck
close the door with a special damn slam
walk away without turning
the key on the deadbolt lock

Chapter 2
The Romance Between Us

Junior Baby sit on his porch
telescoping up & down the street
for his nephew to come pick him up to run errands
he crosshair on three teenaged boys
laughing side-by-side down the sidewalk
tallest buddy in the middle resting his arms
on the shoulders of his two Homies
happiness is a grasshopper jumping all around them
Junior Baby love to see my sons stepping close
ignoring & changing the world at the same time
he look at his watch
got some time
go back in the house
turn on his tape recorder
talk out the second chapter
of his autobiography
HAND ME MY GRIOT CLOTHES:

If you stop look & listen
you can't help but see
the romance between us
flying like tickertape at a parade
linking private love with public touch
man & woman clinking foreheads over love's news
mothers wiping stuff out babychild's eyes
daddy rotating boy or girl so they face the world

or teenyboppers leaning & scheming till
sidewalks ripple in the heat of their enthusiasm
jumpstarting everybody they meet
everybody who aint looking at them
like they was flickering off TV mug shots

the real romance between us
don't come packaged with fine print rules & directions
aint no formula instant mix iron-on patch of ingredients
that make three young black boys
walk down the street like a silly-stepping storm
close enough to stand each other up
friend enough to smell each other's hamburger breath
like it was a family thing
the real romance walk the fine line
between owning up and ownership

not like that man I saw on a downtown sidewalk
leaning hands on knees
up close to a woman walking lunchbreak
minding her own business & him leering
damn near up her dress & black stockings
grunting down in the mud like she supposed
to find chills & thrills in the sound

what make a grown man disforget the righteous tip
of a polite nod or a sweet timestopping opening line
might make a smile erase the citymask
& ignite a short two-way between strangers
who win each other's attention
what make a grown man disremember how to raise
himself tall enough to see into the eyes of John Henry
or other such common sense swingers
full of heroic stories and Comparison
he don't own his own self & he up there trying to
own the whole sidewalk without a permit
staking claim with ignorance & insult
taking somebody's time & dignity
without bringing not even a sign about
the world coming to an end
or charging the government with genocide or saying
down with junk bonds & corporate raiders riding off
into the economic sunset

I never wanted to own no man woman or child
I didn't need no power over nobody
to make me feel like a man
but I always owned up
when I loved some man woman child
& I worked with some men in my day
men I loved men who shoulders I leaned on
men who knew they could turn their backs on me
men who owned wisdom
& knowledge of how to do things
like hard work with heavy machines
like knowing when to stand up tall & look another
lover man woman or child eye to eye
when to cut their eyes at any other man want to raise
himself standing on somebody else's sweaty bent back
I knew some men work at high noon
without grumble groan or grunt & still be willing to
pass their secret style onto a newcoming younger Blood
trying but just aint got the hang of it yet
handing off as much as he could handle
till he finally learn the password
open the way to doin the do

them young boys found their way
handing off friendship like one them relay teams
whoever need it most
get a smile get a hand on the shoulder
get a ear a nod a frown if the news is sad
a grin if the joke supposed to punchline

hand me my griot clothes
I'm changing everybody I meet from now on
all by myself I'm romancing the planet
all by myself I'm raising baby storms
into full grown men
aint no bout a doubt it
I'm carrying spells in the bags of my eyes

hypnotizing man woman child
snap my fingers & lightning flash
make whole people electric

half people whole & ready
to testify about the spin they going to put on the world

from now on I'm waving my hands magical & snaky
up in front of glazed eyes
pumping out people's need
replacing it with romance & a post hypnotic
suggestion to pass it on everytime they see
a confused young man everytime they see
daughter think she aint beautiful everytime they hear
a rapper go 'Yo Bitch!'
they'll kick that romance in
like Larry Graham on bass
thick & rich
chocolate as the complexion
on that tall black boy walking
with his partners down my sidewalk
chunky & full of menthol so cool
we won't never need a pack of Kool again

hand me my griot clothes
I'm changing everybody I meet from now on
I'm changing everybody I meet from now on
I don't want to own nobody
(I don't want the responsibility)
but I will chance the romance between us
I will chant the romance between us

repeating myself
repeating myself

till I break up the congestion
locking vinegar in our blood
till I got respect hiphopping

    in out
    between & beside
    up & down
the sidewalks winding
through the neighborhoods stretching
past the horizons of all our hungry lives

Junior Baby hear the car horn
he turn off the tape recorder
press the rewind button
walk out on the porch
wave to his nephew
lock the door behind him
glance up & down the sidewalk
the kids gone about their business
left the concrete menthol & romantic
Junior Baby walk down the stairs
got a lot of rounds to make
on a bright young Saturday

Chapter 3
This Group Name Rufus

Junior Baby riding with his nephew
radio hollers all kinds of songs
New Jack Swing got the upholstery breathing
Hip Hop samples age-old James Brown
DJ say remember this group name Rufus?
back when Chaka Khan was unknown & full of fire
streaking out her mouth & straight into neon?
Junior Baby get this remember look on his face
turn up the volume till synthesizers & guitar
echo Once You Get Started
Junior Baby finally return home
go to his music room without even
taking off his jacket
pull out his Rufus album
got Ain't Nobody on it
put the LP on the turntable
don't play it yet
go push the record button on his tape recorder
sit down & begin the next chapter
of his autobiography
HAND ME MY GRIOT CLOTHES
start singsong dictating:

I got to hand it to God
Chaka's voice got comets flying from it
don't sound like nobody no thing
anywhere else I ever heard
except maybe a newborn baby found out
all it got to do is wail awhile
to bring adults running upside the crib
hugs full of rock & coo & lullaby
to calm down the whole wide world

when Rufus first start
wasn't nobody really set aside starlike
but DJs producers & everyday people
heard that girl's voice & wasn't nothing
but another album before big colored letters
shouted Rufus featuring Chaka Khan
featuring her newbaby voice snaking
in & out the music
on & off the beat
making everybody forget they didn't know
how the hell an American music band
got a name like Rufus
that make them think of anonymous namebrands
sweating amazing acrobatics on stage
till they hopskip up to top billing
proudly dressed in rhinestone studded
ready willing & able
somebody like Rufus Thomas
wearing pink cape & hot pants
dancing in front of thousands of hundreds of
natural wearing fans rocking
at Wattstax in LA or Soul to Soul in Chicago
everybody clucking Rufus on while he up there
singing about funky chickens & penguins
awkward stalking from one side
of the bandstand to the other
hitching & kicking his satin-covered
matching platform shoes
without missing not one single beat

Rufus Thomas clip clopping his Breakdown
wasn't nothing but ancient memory
taking flight & flesh across the Atlantic
up from Memphis & lightfoot landing on the
American stage in full daylight or spotlight
so that me & you could unchain ourselves

from the jerk & boogaloo as danced
on American Bandstand or Hullabaloo
whitewatered
no *whitewashed*
cause the thing I like about white water
is that it's wild & spitting
slamming & dragging rocks under the surface
draining currents into whirlpools & always
overturning canoe raft rowboat or kayak
silly enough to ride its waves
the Funky Chicken the Mashed Potatoes
& all them other dances flying
out from our imaginative feet
aint nothing but creative sweat
frothing off the face of grand rapids
from the Nile or the Mississippi or the Potomac

hand me my griot clothes
cause Chaka's voice splash in my ears
just dripping with rapids
only a group name Rufus
could feature a sound like Chaka Khan
only a name like Rufus featuring Chaka Khan
could make you think of something
raw & full of that spirit
send them people into the hills of Jamaica
or back upriver in Suriname
& call themselves Maroons
& dare 'ner slave holder
come into town & try *just try*
to take them back
to sugar cane plantations or breeding rooms
only a name like Chaka Khan " featuring Rufus "
could include a voice still remember
the volume of millions
laying underneath the Atlantic Ocean

dove off the decks of slave ships
or died as heroic mutineers
rather than sit packed in shit & spit & vomit
& inevitable sale where the water
lapped up on lush islands speaking
European patois made out the sound
of murdered societies been around up & down
& finding their own style
hundreds of years before Columbus got lost

hand me my griot clothes
see, Chaka would have been a warning
so we could hide fight unify
she rose up from the Great Rift Valley
stepped across cataracts of the Nile
climbed then straddled the Pyramid's tip
she would have sang
the British were coming/the British were coming
eyes glowing revolving beacons into the future
sang the evil were coming/the evil were coming
hands soul-clapping percussion of resistance
sang the myth-makers were coming/
the myth-makers were coming
hips rocking shifting inside the downbeat of remembrance

I know Chaka touch the Rufus dancing in all of us
                    Chaka can Chaka can

Chaka's song melted & seeped
into the mud we found ourselves dragged through
on the way to Long Water
it dried with the crusty earth on our skin
every time we need her whitewater holler
it churns up the bloodstream
Chaka is heart medicine
for a continent full of people name Rufus
an invisible patch of antibiotic timbre

Chaka is a musical smoke that thunders*
opening her mouth to honor
the waterlogged promises
the secret messages
the stunning languages
that dilute our misery
our misery becoming fainter & fainter
till it's used only as food for thought
by people who got ready
caught the train that's coming
people who made ready willing & able
visible on the uncracked masks of our shining real faces
& in the breakdown of our widely imitated walk & talk
aint nothing but a maybe/I sure would like to know

Junior Baby turn off the tape recorder
push the rewind button
go face to face with the turntable
drop the needle on the record
Aint Nobody bubble through the speakers
Junior Baby shift his hips inside the beat of remembrance
roll up his sleeve to take his medicine like a man!

*Mosi-ao-tunya —the Kololo people's name for so-called
"Lake Victoria" in Zimbabwe when David Livingstone
named the waterfall in 1855.

Chapter 4
What It Mean To Be 16

*Junior Baby reading the paper
after Nelson Mandela released
different stories round up opinions
about the effects of Mandela walking
hand-in-hand with Winnie after 27 years
"Afrikaners Feel Betrayed by de Klerk"
one headline say   another story say the
"special covert army unit called the
Civil Cooperation Bureau" set up
"to infiltrate anti-apartheid
and black nationalist groups"
was under investigation for murdering
two white anti-apartheid activists
Junior Baby put down the paper
he can't stand lies coated with innocence
he figure divine white nations
& civil cooperation bureaus
go together like snuff & Listerine
like republic & South Africa
Junior Baby turn on his tape recorder
start the next chapter of his autobiography*
HAND ME MY GRIOT CLOTHES
start dictating:

I f my daddy heard Afrikaners mixing
civil with *cooperation* he probably say
what he told me when I was 16
& trying to be a man too soon
 you can't have your cake & eat it too
for a long time I couldn't
lick the meaning off that 9-word lecture
but now I see what daddy was saying:

Afrikaners want the new constitution
fresh baked to suit boiled potato tastes
after their chefs banned Mandela the cayenne
out the legal stanzas all these years
at 16 I missed his point up one side & down the other
I remember snotting & crying & pouting
after daddy & ma found out I was sniffing around
a 24-year-old woman & made me go tell her
I couldn't be around her no more
pops told me
you aint grown because you think you grown
becoming a man mean putting your whole life on layaway
& never getting back even half what you put down

he say
you may got the equipment that a man got
but you don't know the power you messing with
you aint nothing but a boy
that woman
sized you up stripped you down ate you up
before you ever knew what hit you
you may read your biology books & centerfolds
maybe even hugged & rubbed & tapped
a few asses here & there
but I know what you *think* you know
he was right
was no way shape or form for me to know
armed only with teenaged whispers
that the first time should be older
with somebody teaching you the moves
& unwrapping you like a melting popsicle

I thought you just went to the Layaway Window
& withdrew the man you needed or wanted to be
Shaft or Superman or Superfly
private eye indestructible slickbacked lovers
sticking deep riding with a rockinghorse groove

all the while eyeing the souped up getaway car
or red white & blue tights idling in the cut
till I got ready to go
I finally realized
you aint never ready to go
you always want a clause in the constitution
when the getting is good as the first time
when the fields are plowed seeded harvested
& shipped for your leisure
when the loving don't come
from two-handed understanding
when the wealth fills your head & history with power
you always want your cake & eat it too

I'm in love I told daddy & ma
you can't tell me what I feel
I'm the president of the Civil Cooperation Bureau
you trespassing on my time
I didn't know I got addicted
until I got to be adult myself
& go around come around result in having children
with that same woman six years later
(so damn determined to taste cake & eat it too!)
I watched our son peek 16 only to get mad
wondering which parent's memory would guide us
if the fantasies of some older woman
stalked the dimpled puberty of our version of me
you better bet I planned on kicking ass
& jangling the keys of closing cell doors
after a due-time presentation
complete with names places & testimony

hand me my griot clothes
I don't believe in stealing childhood
I don't believe she ever loved me
I don't believe apartheid is civil
I don't believe my son is Shaft

I know what it mean to be 16
being cake & ate up too
having my body make a promise
my heart couldn't keep
hearing a woman's voice echo in my ears
when all I could handle was a Shirelle's *Who Said/She Said*
I know the dangers of using big words too soon
strutting to definitions best understood
only when you naturally out on your own
trusting high school biology
when you really need a chemistry Ph.D

hand me my griot clothes
silencing a boy's youth using guerilla sex
radioactive sweet talk & exaggerated satisfaction
the same as
snatching people's land using guerilla bibles
trapdoor treaties & international finance
aint no difference between a human & a country
use up the human
speed up the emotions & youth
you got exhausted touch
can't reward your passion with joy & change
use up the land
dig out the minerals & fertility
you got mean earth
can't reward your digging with jewels or food

in other words
rape aint seduction
terrorism aint cooperation
I aint never saying I love you to nobody I don't love
I won't touch nobody with push come to shove
I don't reach for hearts don't know how to love

you can't have your cake & eat it too
(I think I got it right daddy)

you can't eat your cake & have it too
(I believe it's coming together ma)

you have your cake but can't eat your too
(nothing beat a failure but a try)

your cake can't have it & eat you too
(say what you mean/mean what you say)

it can't have your cake & eat you too
(fair exchange aint no robbery)

> *Junior Baby turn off the tape recorder*
> *press the rewind button*
> *roll the newspaper stories into a ball*
> *toss it over his head*
> *at the garbage can behind his back*
> *he know he scored without even looking*
> *the 16-year-old point guard inside*
> *tell him it's alright*
> *it's alright it's alright*

Chapter 5
Some Beautiful Action

Junior Baby overheard a young Blood
greet a buddy on the Metro:
you with the UZI in your briefcase....
let's go stick up Sears.
Junior Baby sucked his teeth
at such classic lack of vision
didn't turn around but when he got home
turned on his tape recorder
started the next chapter
of his autobiography
HAND ME MY GRIOT CLOTHES
start dictating:

I been young & wild too
chewing words of violence
like a redneck tonguing sticks of straw
we cussed so much in Junior High
we got guilty & made up The Cussing Game
trying to make each other act right in public
simple rules: anybody hear anybody else
saying M.F. or shit or Goddamn or
Black Ass M.F. or any solo combination
got a free steal dead in the chest
I got stole so hard once
I fell off the curb
almost got run over by a PEPCO truck
coulda made a video off the steps I danced
to get my narrow ass out the way
my boys laughed like a sister
had just told me no at a GoGo

times different now
cussing the tip of the iceberg
anytime somebody talking about pulling
UZIs out a briefcase on a public subway
it's a funny thing about that cussing game
it didn't stop nobody from cussing really
but we knew cussing loud & wrong was wrong
so hitting a buddy gave some due
to the adult stirring inside us
a man peeked out our young boys' eyes
breaking rules & setting them at the same time
I heard that in young Blood's voice
talking about sticking up a Sears
to steal what?
some Goddamn Craftsman tools?
shoot who?
some other young soul
tightroping between hip and square?

hand me my griot clothes
(threatening a department store!)

make me think of James Brown & Bobby Byrd
 like a dull knife/just aint cutting/
 talking loud/saying nothing
I'm so tired of hearing somebody
                all breathless & shit
                all confidential & shit
                all say & no show

say but make the thing the real thing
aint nothing like the real thing
I know who got the threat of death
who got the Beautiful Action
we need the Beautiful Action
some friction of words becoming deeds
right before our eyes   some briefcase documenting

cold-blooded accomplishments   some promises sweating
into monuments we could take our children to
I know who got the threat of a bullet in the chest
who steady honing the touch of wealth all over the body
who climbing out the rut of good intentions
with wind chimes strapped like a bandolera cross the chest
who aching from pushing/pulling
Beautiful Action uphill in this world
sermons from the pulpit or soapbox
sacred in their own right/calling out right
against wrong worth the sound it makes
(such testifying can move the National Mind)
but without Beautiful Action
it's body without spirit

I swear I don't mean to ride my High Horse
but when you hear your young brother
courting an early grave
cause he like the clickclack
a bullet make shifting into the barrel of a gun
really aint no more time for subtlety

if his little junior baby ass was mine
I'd whip his behind
then hug all the tears he feel like crying
then take him to the mountains
swim with him in the ocean
play him Paul Robeson records
take him to Africa and Mexico and Jamaica
help him learn Wolof Español and 'Ey Mon
so we can cuss out Christopher Columbus
George Washington Alexander the Great
Napoleon and all them fake ass heros
we get taught like wasn't no action
wearing our history stamp of approval

& I'd listen to him when he spoke
about how he want the world to be
sometimes/a lot of times I bet/
I know he'd try to sneaksay M.F. around me
but I wouldn't hit him in the chest
I'd introduce him to his mother
we'd learn a new word
that could slap somebody who might need it
but without forgetting who brought us in this world

when I wear these griot clothes
when I wear these griot clothes
get me in the mind to preach
to say something good for the world to remember

when I wear these griot clothes
when I wear these griot clothes
I got to stand up & take a step
& everything I do got to have
Beautiful Action in mind
everything I do got to be funky

Junior Baby turn off the tape recorder
push the rewind button
hang up his gray Dob next to his Kufi
hang up his silk suit next to his dashiki
put the blue suede wingtips next to the Ashanti sandals
close the closet door
he pause just long enough
to remember which pocket
he left his Metro ticket in

Chapter 6
I Don't Need No Jewelries

Junior Baby answer the ringing phone
his Nigerian tailor calling from Maryland
say he finished sewing the Mudcloth jacket
how it look? Junior Baby ask
it looks good. it's the best I've made yet
tailor's voice accented with Lagos & Takoma Park
Junior Baby say he can't come get it right now
promise to pick up the jacket soon
clothes on his mind sometime later
when this husky brother get on the Metro
wearing black slip-on shoes with bows on the front
blue socks winking red/green polka dots
to match the green/tan/purple & red ones
blinking across the face of his black shirt
Junior Baby think about style
as he sit down to start the next chapter
of his autobiography
HAND ME MY GRIOT CLOTHES
start dictating:

It's a blessing when you find the style
you can speak without no extra tutoring
it's a blessing when you got your life down
to the rhythm of your own heart
open up your mouth everybody know who speaking
against the grain or shouting amen with the chorus
off the rack or wearing hand-picked stitching
facing the world with a mind of your own
believing in the movement that reveals your soul

once I heard this live album got Sylvester
singing Patti's *You Are My Friend*

Sylvester screamed falsetto up to the break
introduced Two Tons of Fun to the L.P. audience
revealed pure love for his back-up singers
this was before Sylvester died of AIDS
way before Two Tons became Weather Girls
Sylvester testified over a vamping orchestra:
these women can sing yall ...
they don't need these dresses
they don't need them jewelries
they don't need that hair
these women can sing yall

Martha & Izora opened their mouths & proved him right
gave me chills so big I remembered them years later
at a party with some of my Pan Africanist friends
the groove had settled into Name That Tune
by the time I found Sylvester's album
laying in a colorful stack of all kinds of goodies
yall got to hear Sylvester sing *You Are My Friend*
while I spread vinyl on the turntable somebody cracked
Sylvester? aint he that gay Blood from San Francisco?
but it didn't matter one bit
that gay Blood & Martha & Izora
called out the gospel inside that room
Sylvester reclaimed his place at the party
among the brothers & sisters guarding against
all *Who Say/Who Be* that deviated from
the sexual common good agreed upon in that room
which was the only proper way to be you ask me
no I aint never loved another man mouth-to-mouth
never been swept off my feet by no man I ever met
but I played Sylvester at that party & wasn't worried
one way or the other about somebody lining me up
on their seamy right from wrong
I knew Sylvester's voice could satisfy
the moment of our community

he didn't need no jewelries either
no stage lights or even a roomful of advance understanding
that man could sing yall

hand me my griot clothes
I'm still a witness to the power of the Right Decision
still claiming the moment & choosing the beat of my heart
still leaping over somebody else's uncut expectations
still standing against gossip on my own two feet
I can accept praise & inclusion if they real
even crave that membership every once in awhile
but I don't need high fives if I got to step
splat into the Okeedoke to feel the sting

if a Hefty Bag-sized brother bold enough
to wear sweet colored dots on his clothes
I got to notice him with a open & loving set of eyes
it wasn't about honoring his outside in either
the well tailored gold Baggies & leather belt
the amber Gucci leather carrying case
or the slick watch containing more gold
than time-telling numbers on its face
fact is brother wasn't wearing my style at all
it was his personal code & mission I picked up on
he discovered a style & mined it
he carved a style & staged it
that man is a natural resource the way I see it
a 24-carat piece of genuine work
qualified for imitation
but so damn unpredictable he won't stand still
for the poachers aiming at his restless qualifications
I like it when we hold our own like that
even if some judges rule our style is criminal
certain newspapers report that it threatens women
on city streets & some of us become outlaws who
bogard praise backtalk sweettalk & wear a bad name
like it's a pair of two left shoes

hand me my griot clothes
let's get one thing straight though
don't no hoodlums make me doubt myself
whether they sit on the Supreme Court or look out
for business from the balcony of a crack house
aint no outside changing same
tell me whether my style in or out
it could be climbing out the side of a rented limousine
or preaching salvation from a hand-carved soap box

till Mickey Mouse become a Baptist pastor
or Wile E. Coyote become a vegetarian pacifist
till Mr. Spock hit on Lt. Uhura with a get-over line
or Elvis come back as Otis Redding
I will mix polka dots with Mudcloth if I want to
slip on some bow-tied shoes
underneath a new pair of jeans
play Sylvester for nationalists at a house party
enroll my children in an Afrocentric school
I will be a source of energy for this world
I will love the sound of tradition but whip out
a creation story from my own pocket
when I get good & goddamn ready
I will carry myself around like I belong in this world

I aint letting go of nothing if it feed me
I love anything if it free me
I open my mouth to say healing things in language
come full of candid incense & style come beautiful
for every season of the year
like I said
I don't need no jewelries
only this little light of mine
flashing like diamonds come rain or come shine

Junior Baby turn off the tape recorder
press the rewind button
he dial the phone to call the tailor
make appointment to pick up his custom fit jacket
can't wait to wear it out in public
he remember the white marks crisscrossing black Mudcloth
they send real messages back home in Africa
you sure I aint going to be cussing nobody out?
tailor admit he can't translate word-for-word
but he promise the jacket won't embarrass a soul
they hang up after setting a date
Junior Baby wish he knew the language of his clothes
but decide he will be speaking loud & clear
& definitely saying exactly what's on his mind

Chapter 7
You Got To Wear Grief

Junior Baby lay awake tired in his hotel bed
woman's sobs soak the room next door
weeping leaks through the walls
stranger's grief send Junior Baby to a chair
at the round table over by the window
he pull back the curtain & choose neon over 60-watt
night lights reflect off his own grief's memories
stranger's tears sting his mind like a front desk bell
Junior Baby answer the ping
with the next chapter of his autobiography
HAND ME MY GRIOT CLOTHES
he turn on his tape recorder
whisper lessons for all lonely hearts:

You got to wear grief
    if you really want to get over it
stitch your sorrow into silk
custom make it
fit right into the ifs ands or buts
grief is heavy clothes
a snowsuit in July
really aint nothing to do
but overheat & sweat that fever out your system
feel all that pain
claim all that pain
lick tears that sneak up
in the steam of a hot bath
that seep out you
at the peak of a movie scene
let all grief feed your mourning

remember the mother died at 54
remember the father collapsed before reunion
remember childhood friend killed by hotriders
remember lovers used your fever
to key loving someone else
remember King's bitter Lorraine
remember Malcolm's plywood podium
remember unclaimed children floating in supermarket milk
remember middle men & Middle Passage

you got to wear grief
grief aint always wearing black hat & veil either
grief can break you down until you wind up
forgetting what you got on
oversleeping in mismatched socks
make you think style start
with hand-me-down straitjackets
sewn from cheap memories
half-assed ifs ands or buts
and the worn grooves of old Motown 45s

you got to wear grief
you got to wear grief

hand me my griot clothes
listening to overnight sadness
got me owning up
got me shoving open mikes
in front the Aretha inside me
calling out to Sweet Inspirations
always in the background
whenever I come clean with myself
I know the girl's tears
I know she aint being general
she laying there missing
particular touch right there

particular kiss right here
understanding voice in times of need

me & her know about happiness
that's why we know about grief
see, happiness is naked
laying next to somebody loving skin to skin
happiness is naked
saying up next to somebody soul to soul
happiness is naked
waiting for somebody way past a decent hour
happiness is light & silly
a child acting grown
old man giggling babylike
happiness is wearing hip black clothes
standing beside Barry White at the Grammys
a strip of Kente peeking from under your collar
happiness pick up all awards
provide all rewards
happiness is independence
late night/all night phone calls
happiness unbutton overcoats & disregard The Hawk
happiness lose gloves between seats on the subway
happiness walk outside right after a hot shower
happiness thigh-tie scarves like Hendrix onstage

but if you wear black
you got to expect some lint
every once in a while
I know what I miss
she sat on my face
I sat on hers
I called her name
she called my name
we kissed for hours
fell asleep in each other's arms
seduced longdistance

set up interstate rendezvous
caught first-run movies
gotaway some weekends
kept each other awake after latenight wrong turns
unlocked the recipe to making pancakes from scratch
stood toe to toe about right & wrong
then laughed when argument got silly
broke up
patched up
slowdragged to Lionel Richie & the O'Jays Live
had our names mispronounced over PA systems
& answered anyway cause the echo
made us sound like runaway movie stars

hand me my griot clothes
go head
cry it all out girl
I don't even need to know your name
or the everydays about your pain
I am a witness though
hearing you got me listening to myself
nodding my head to the back beat
of Aretha singing *Sweet Bitter Love*
refusing to hold back the flood
of my own tearsoaked reasons for solitude
wear your grief girl
I'm wearing mine
the sun might find us puffy-eyed
but we'll be closer to happiness
having gave it up tonight
I'll wave to you
if we pass by each other
on the way home tomorrow
I'll know you by the shine in your step
you'll know me by my black leather jacket

I'll be the one flicking
a mannish piece of lint off my shoulder

> *Junior Baby turn off the tape recorder*
> *push the rewind button*
> *close his eyes and listen*
> *she must have cried herself to sleep*
> *Junior Baby get back in bed*
> *close his eyes*
> *night lights reflect off his own sleep's tears*

Chapter 8
The Danger of Thinking Either/Or

Junior Baby walk into the elevator
three women already standing inside the closing doors
two coworkers stand together
sister worker wear her hair straight
Asian worker wear her hair natural
other sister to his left got her hair in braids
your hair look nice Junior Baby tell her
she smile a quiet thank you
he always been partial to that African look
even learned how to braid his own daughter's hair
I guess our hair doesn't look good
sister worker deadpan to Asian worker
air get thick in the elevator
Junior Baby meet the crack head on
see, that's that either/or trap he say
elevator doors open & the women leave first
Junior Baby walk out by himself
stick to his compliment & his principles
decide later to start the next
chapter of his autobiography
HAND ME MY GRIOT CLOTHES
dictate why he got no use for thinking either/or:

I don't know why she tried putting
her words in my mouth like that
I was polite to her
we smiled elevator friendly
to smooth the trip down eight floors
then I saw them braids
imagined two-handed butterflies
custom combing sheen up & down the parts
in that woman's hair & I had to give it up

braiding just give me a special feeling
ever since I learned how to plait my babygirl's hair
I never did press perm or process her hair
plus all the women I ever loved like a man
had thick hair alive with historical & fragrant styles
facing off against TV blonds on billboards
& inside the covers of magazines
but I aint never been about dogging some other sister
who do perm hot comb or tease a pony tail
down one side her head or starch the other side tall
with adventurous gel or dramatic mousse

as a boy all my mothers had straight hair
I loved every one of them too
women who birthed me or raised me
asked for hugs & pecks full of sugar on the cheeks
smelling of pancake make-up & Breck hairspray
staking their claims on me with strong perfumes
smacks on my behind & snacks after school
they still stand for beauty in my life
tinted with sepia in my memories
proudly smiling at the pride I took using a
black hard-rubber comb & hair dressing on my
frowning teary-eyed daughter fidgeting under tender scalp

I'm saying I'm tired of the either/or thing
simplistic thinking in a 2+2 style when we got to get
comfortable with multiplication divided by heart & soul
I can't use simple minded slogans no more like
 if you aint part of the solution you part of the problem
stick that mess in a mass-produced Chinese cookie
it give somebody a bad case of heartburn

if it's really deep
forget wrapping it up in crumbling Short & Sweet
unless you auditioning for the evening news spotlight
if it's giving a million people the blues

forget stir frying the Rhythms of Salvation
unless you trying to feed world hunger with appetizers
if it's deep forget
forgetting about everybody else's ideas dreams & solutions
unless you trying to wear the only crown defining
what is hip

that's the danger of thinking either/or
that's the danger of one person movement or style
wearing robes or uniforms stitched from virgin fabric
promising convenient handles for lazy minds
enforcing territorial whims with snarling cliches
you wind up with a monopoly on what is hip
guarded by paramilitary disciples & groupies

I read somewhere that scientists say
we only use a finger snap's worth of our brain power
that if we put our minds to it
there aint nothing we can't learn
nothing foreign that can't become habit
no way of thinking no behavior no language
the mind can't stretch to understand
if we don't decide that what we already know
is all we'll ever need to know

hand me my griot clothes
a man or woman aint special
because they possess the Grand Wisdom
what's special is their spice their spin
the terrible originality each one can bring
each one memorable & always able to start a trend
begin by peeling up tradition's edges
finish by pasting them back down at the feet
of another person waiting to unpeel one-of-a-kind genius
not manipulating nobody
faking like you want to hear what's on their mind
only to shout treason soon as they take a deep breath

but inspiring somebody
encouraging them to go beyond the seen & heard
till they crack into the sweet marrow of lasting contribution
sometimes disagreeing sure but not dehumanizing nobody
not disassembling or dissecting without remembering
the humane blueprint for reconstruction that make
everybody feel like they rippling with invention

hand me my griot clothes
I aint part of the solution
but I aint part of the problem either
I aint part of no one thing don't let me think
or listen to the sound of other folks thinking
I aint thinking either/or no more
I'm thinking like GoGo musicians
standing on the bandstand for hours at a time
if it take that long to hear yall out
calling for all the help I need
to pump out a molasses groove rock the whole house
with cowbells timbales & generosity thick in the mix
GoGo players say that'll work/that'll work
as a brother conga drumming hiphop on the stage
as a sister click clacking sticks pop into the spot
as Chuck Brown feedback Duke Ellington
through the system
as a vocalist slur some Ohio Players during the solo

that'll work/that'll work
as somebody thinking about reparations stand up
as somebody talk suit & tie look out for Number 1
as some man spouting mystic wishes chant some praise
as some woman claiming victim status cast her vote
or as some whole nother neverheard voice
peep up from way in the back row

no I aint giving no play to out & out traitors
selling their mothers to the highest bidder

pointing out their fathers to the hit man on the sly
calling children ugly hiding mirrors behind their backs
but if you somebody otherwise living right
making some beauty where they aint none
standing against orders that you sit tight
that'll work as far as I'm concerned

the genuine thing the thoughtful thing
coming from the heart mind & soul
or from invisible places where happy live
or even that place you visit
when you sleeping on the sofa
during the Lakers & Pistons seventh game
all that'll work & it'll be so good to go
I got to laugh wondering how I ever thought
thinking either/or made any damn sense at all

Junior Baby turn off the tape recorder
press the rewind button
he hope elevator woman didn't take it personal
but he really do like when women
wear their braids & dreads & naturals
even as he still love a whiff
of his mothers' talcum powdered styles
Junior Baby expect she need to compliment her own self
let go that static clinging either/or
get busy living large with
everything is everything
all 'n all
I & I
Junior Baby nod his head & think
that'll work
sho you right
that will definitely work

Chapter 9
Life Aint No Product

one day Junior Baby go to the daycare center
with his friend the second-time father in his 40s
he shotgun in the VW bus while father & son talk
the 6-year-old full of questions
the grown man full of answers
another day Junior Baby walk behind a young mother
happily carrying her overgrown son to the bus stop
the boy ride her right hip & hug her neck
the woman strain with her joyful burden
Junior Baby notice how both woman & man calmly absorb
the sparks shooting out their children's mouths
father & mother like giants in their children's eyes
full of mysterious patience & answers to all-size wonders
Junior Baby remember the love he witness
when he turn on his tape recorder to start
the next chapter of his autobiography
HAND ME MY GRIOT CLOTHES
he think out loud:

I know people hug their children everyday
but sometime itty bitty scenes of love slow me down
make me feel like I'm walking in space
& staring into sacred scenery
remind me of a picture I seen once
looking from earth into the center of the Milky Way
black background red lights with stars blazing white
make me realize the world may look little
trapped by visions of turf on our side of town
& all that borderline stalking
but what look little is really too big too see
if you too close up on top of it
witnessing them tiny big moments of love

the way I get to see life & feel the planet
move in the windless orbit of my bones
it don't matter whether I see single or married parents
a commuter showing a blind man into the subway
a cub scout leader guiding babies into boys
or somebody unofficially counseling
boys into men or girls into women
it's a slice of life pick me up & make me pass it on

tell you the honest-to-goodness truth
I get so tired hearing about children need
positive role models & images standing
professional & tall with starch & creases
children don't need nobody's *idea* of a good person
got his picture on a government I.D. or corporate paycheck
children don't care if you Raggedy Ann or Andy

long as you listen when they talk
watch when they walk
hug when they fall
stern when they stall
anybody hip don't let them give into the
uncooperative *My Way* living like a virus in all us
anybody hip demonstrating love & living the hero they need
laughing till they know a good punchline
when they hear it
crying when the grief is real
anybody hip got the abracadabra when they whine
change that manipulation into conversation
till they can say the world sincerely
from the bottom of their own imaginations

role models & positive images
nuclear families & broken homes
single parents & rolling stones
life aint no damn product
that's why it's no deposit no return

too many people aint hip because they forever
stringing life up with words
like they was butchers cutting off excess fat
trimming the possibilities off a median
income or a real estate assessment
putting a person on the scale off the way
a person talk or whether a man in the home
or a woman got babies by more than one father
everybody look the same on X-rays
it aint about coming to conclusions all the time
everyday people go from devil to god
or they be devil in the morning see a baby smile
on the bus at lunchtime get back to being devil
at supper but feel that seed smiling like an infant
waiting for the right time to come alive
babies live inside every grown up anyway
we all got a womb if we think about it
we can give birth to danger or adventure or wisdom
we can be the proud parents of a sense of honor
just as easy as a plan to carve up Africa
we can find a sense of humor in Dracula's face
holler at him like Richard Pryor's wino did
make him think twice before
he break in somebody's window

hand me my griot clothes
life aint no formula
life is Top 40 rock & roll soul
jazz classical & New Wave music all rolled
up & down the scale the way Little Richard
would play the sound track if we billions
asked him to play the song to go alongside our 24 hours

I know there got to be definitions sometimes
I aint hollering for uncivilization
I aint demanding the right to discover & conquer
somebody's land just because my science

aint allowed me to hear about it yet
I aint demanding the right to yell fire in the movie house
to giggle while people trampling over each other in panic
I know love get translated by a firm hand every now & then
even the planet got its own path following universal rules
elected by the unseen democracy of nature
I'm saying get rid of the formfitting fears strapping
life down & the dressed up lies limiting people's minds

hand me my griot clothes
life can't be test marketed & fine tuned
to match the results from national surveys
of select group samples from little towns sitting
far inside themselves
but way out of touch with changing times
camping out in isolation is what tribes do
find steady water mark down borders
kill visitors with different sounds or dress
then convince themselves that death is right on time
life is about the ties that bind
holding hands with the child in you
ready to learn new sounds or dress or another lesson
ready to play games with old rules new rules
or none at all long as don't nobody
get hurt or feel like a stranger

my eyes aint big enough to see all of life
what a thing to finally know
I don't have to worry about how life going to end
I'm just a day-to-day caretaker of the human spirit
my only job is learning to speak the language of creativity
there's a Crying Man in my dreams
upset because he know he got to die
that's the only product I know I got to buy
me & the Crying Man got an understanding
when the product of my life is finally manufactured
it's going to be/it's *got* to be

full of general style humane wit occasional blues
& insistent toleration for most other folks
not to mention bold face memories
worth retelling by satellites zigzagging
breathless toward the North Star
& ideas became deeds echoed among the quasars
by riffing Little Richard's billion-selling soundtrack

Junior Baby turn off the tape recorder
push the rewind button
remember what Billy Preston said
nothing from nothing leave nothing
he turn off the lights
wonder what the Crying Man will say to that
probably something deep like
death is the common denominator
Junior Baby chuckle & think
yeah but life can't never be subtracted

Chapter 10
Like A Human Being

Junior Baby wait on a red light in Georgetown
Homeless Man's necksign say I'm hungry
Homeless Man hold out his cup
Junior Baby say I aint got it today brother
Homeless Man cup toward other people on the corner
he turn back to Junior Baby
this man got mad at me cause I wouldn't
eat this food he brought me.... I don't eat pork.
Junior Baby had to accept that
the light flash red to green
Junior Baby washed by the stampeding crowd
he shake the Homeless Man's hand before wading himself
Homeless Man's voice follow Junior Baby rest of the day
till he get home
turn on his tape recorder
start the next chapter of his autobiography
HAND ME MY GRIOT CLOTHES
he start dictating:

I can just see him
mad & disgusted
staring in that homeless human's face
dripping questions off his tongue
like he was a short order cook
emptying day-old Crisco

what you mean you don't eat no pork?
you a street corner Farrakhan now?
pride aint straightening out them
creases in your empty stomach!

I bet the cat even threw the food down on the ground
right there at the intersection of Wisconsin & M

rather than eat the grease himself
or ask one of the 20-11 other homeless Bloods
camped on concrete Holiday Inns
if they had a taste for some fastfood pork

I guess homeless Homeboy aint supposed to choose
what he want to eat since he pointing a cup at strangers
& on the real side brother did look healthy enough
to head to the union hall or the unemployment office
I admit I sometimes wish I could resist
that flash of get out my face
whenever some man smelling like piss & resignation
up in my face when I'm out walking talking & cooling

but really
you don't have to eat pork
whether you Muslim homeless or not
if you willing to handle the weight of your particulars
I don't have to give up no money just cause he stick that
cup in my face & hand me a Reader's Digest story
I can't take the blame for his situation
I work everyday to make this world a better place
I raise my children & love my family
hold doors open for friends & strangers
smile at babies in supermarkets

I treat everybody I meet like a human being
whether I meet them in the penthouse or on the sidewalk
the more I live
the more people I meet
the more I listen
the more I realize
there aint no higher way to treat somebody
or be treated
no more special way to treat somebody special
than look through your eyes & recognize yourself
in the many faces of babies or Gray Panthers

women or the knee dipping Dions doing their hair
teenagers in a wheelchair or Bo Jackson look-a-likes
Africans Russians or any other faces
angled along the curves
of this third planet from the sun
including a person sleep on a grate
in the United States of America

so when a homeless Black man panhandling
on the corner
say he turned down some one-shot pork chops
that ring a bell of common sense in me
cause if I was homeless
& you was going to give me something
I'd want more than a meal from Denny's
give me a job or some good advice
tell me a damn inspiring story
sing me a verse of *The Way You Do The Things You Do*
or tell me no I aint got penny nickel dime or quarter
for your lazy ass & you just better get out my face

I'd rather hear all that
than have you face me
with a styrofoam container of grit getting cold
like I want you deciding what I want to eat
all I asked for was whatever amount of change
you think you can share
out the goodness of your heart

hand me my griot clothes
there aint no reason why
just cause a man homeless
he can't still decide to look in whoever eyes he want
to maintain his kinship with another human being
he could be standing on that corner
thinking about how Marvin Junior held his breath
for so long on the Dells' *Stay In My Corner*

remembering when he first bought that 45
rushed home   put it on the record player
& closed his eyes on memories of his girlfriend
as they teeny-stepped into a private corner
at a Saturday night party

if I was standing out tattered on the corner
I might be recalling how Gary Alston
flaunted all conventions to become the best
double dutch jumping
hand dance dancing
hopscotch skipping
teenage boy that we ever seen in Parklands
I might be thinking that Gary didn't give a shit about who
thought he was gay or who liked or didn't like him
because by the way Gary could also swing the toughest
tricks on the monkey bars
knock a baseball as far as the big oak tree
standing 50 yards out in center field
& make friends with all the finest women
who I could only look at or jones on
when they passed my way

hand me my griot clothes
like Marvin Junior
Gary Alston & that discriminating
homeless man in Georgetown
I'm choosing as my minimum daily principle
the requirement that I say thank you
when I return from sleep
& swing out into the day on a humane tip
ready to have somebody drink a new way of living
just by sipping the air when I walk on by

I'm claiming a style that lasts awhile
dropping all that class crap
about whose family name carry more tradition

than that person's complexion mixed
with what blood circulated from
that certain part of town

I'm taking the advice of Ashford & Simpson
giving everybody something real
giving everybody some of the long breath of me
giving everybody some of the double dutch of me
giving everybody something they can feel

the Cinque of me mixed with the Idi Amin of me
the AIDS patient of me
hugged by the Mother Hale of me
the Coltrane of me vamped by the
Ladysmith Black Mambazo of me
the Soul Train of me squared by
the Dance Fever of me
the Jefferson Davis of me
subverted by the John Brown of me
the animal of me chasing the philosopher of me

I'm treating human beings like human beings

sometimes you will tempt me to talk about your mother
sometimes you will dare me to talk about your mother
sometimes I promise to talk about your mother
when I can't stand the temptation no longer
but I'll jump bad straight at you one-on-one
not bouncing off a satellite like the CIA NSA or FBI
peeping your bedroom to see who you sucking & rubbing
anyway most times when I can't say nothing good
I might just nod & keep my mouth shut
till you climb up out that hole
ready to drop a coin in a homeless man's cup
or say I don't have it today brother
rather than pointing a cold pork chop in his face
like it was a magic lamp housing a scolding genie
begrudgingly granting one out of three wishes

keep your solos clean & shining
don't nobody need all that signifying
treat the man like a human being
he liable to treat you like one right back at you

Junior Baby turn off the tape recorder
push the rewind button
go look in the freezer for something to eat
got a taste for pork chops
string beans & mashed potatoes
laugh out loud when that cold air hit his face
nothing there but frozen apple juice & waffles
Junior Baby aint ate pork chops since the Sixties
he close the freezer
pull some bean curd & broccoli out the box
he aint no Muslim
but he long ago decided how to eat to live

Peter J. Harris is the author of *Wherever Dreams Live* (Folktales) and *Six Soft Sketches of a Man* (Poetry). He has published poetry in many magazines, including *The Black Scholar* (Oakland, CA), *Blind Alleys* (Baltimore), and *Race Today* (London). He is the founding publisher and editor of *Genetic Dancers, The Magazine for and about the Artistry Within African/American Fathers*. Harris has also published articles and short fiction in several magazines and anthologies including *Essence* magazine and *Breaking Ice: An Anthology of Contemporary African-American Fiction*. From 1979 to 1984, he wrote "SportSoul," a column on sports and culture, for the *Baltimore Afro-American*. He has also been a staff reporter for the Wilmington (DE) *News-Journal* and Assistant Editor of *The Dispatcher*, published by the International Longshoremen's and Warehousemen's Union in San Francisco. A graduate of Howard University (1977, Journalism), Harris was born and raised in Southeast Washington, DC and is the father of three children.